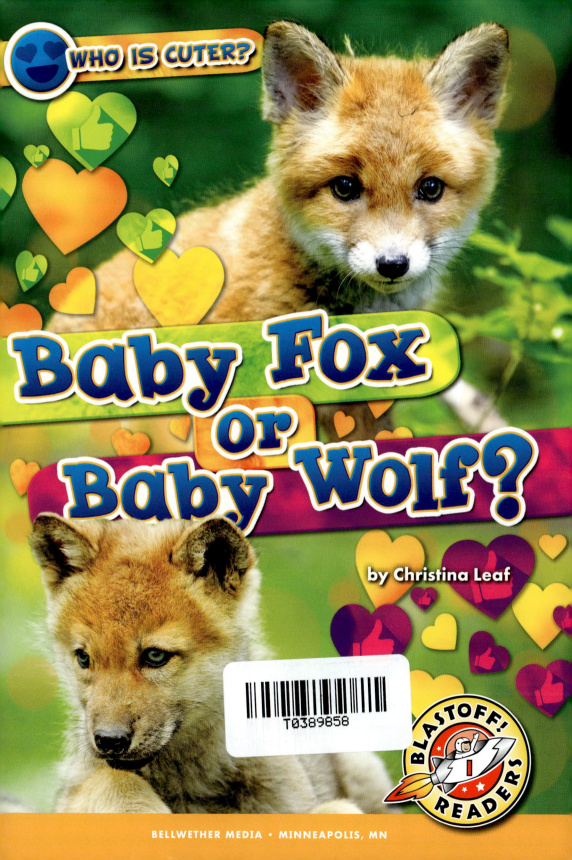

Blastoff! Readers are carefully developed by literacy experts to build reading stamina and move students toward fluency by combining standards-based content with developmentally appropriate text.

LEVELS

Level 1 provides the most support through repetition of high-frequency words, light text, predictable sentence patterns, and strong visual support.

Level 2 offers early readers a bit more challenge through varied sentences, increased text load, and text-supportive special features.

Level 3 advances early-fluent readers toward fluency through increased text load, less reliance on photos, advancing concepts, longer sentences, and more complex special features.

★ Blastoff! Universe

Reading Level

Grade K → Grades 1–3 → Grade 4

This edition first published in 2025 by Bellwether Media, Inc.

No part of this publication may be reproduced in whole or in part without written permission of the publisher. For information regarding permission, write to Bellwether Media, Inc., Attention: Permissions Department, 6012 Blue Circle Drive, Minnetonka, MN 55343.

Library of Congress Cataloging-in-Publication Data

Names: Leaf, Christina, author.
Title: Baby fox or baby wolf? / by Christina Leaf.
Description: Minneapolis, MN : Bellwether Media, Inc., 2025. | Series: Blastoff! readers: who is cuter? | Includes bibliographical references and index. | Audience: Ages 5-8 | Audience: Grades K-1 | Summary: "Developed by literacy experts for students in kindergarten through grade three, this book introduces the differences between baby foxes and baby wolves to young readers through leveled text and related photos"– Provided by publisher.
Identifiers: LCCN 2024003101 (print) | LCCN 2024003102 (ebook) | ISBN 9798886870305 (library binding) | ISBN 9798893041446 (paperback) | ISBN 9781644878743 (ebook)
Subjects: LCSH: Foxes–Juvenile literature. | Wolves–Juvenile literature. | Foxes–Infancy–Juvenile literature. | Wolves–Infancy–Juvenile literature. | Foxes–Behavior–Juvenile literature. | Wolves–Behavior–Juvenile literature.
Classification: LCC QL737.C22 L433 2025 (print) | LCC QL737.C22 (ebook) | DDC 599.773–dc23/eng/20240301
LC record available at https://lccn.loc.gov/2024003101
LC ebook record available at https://lccn.loc.gov/2024003102

Text copyright © 2025 by Bellwether Media, Inc. BLASTOFF! READERS and associated logos are trademarks and/or registered trademarks of Bellwether Media, Inc. Bellwether Media is a division of Chrysalis Education Group.

Editor: Suzane Nguyen   Designer: Andrea Schneider

Printed in the United States of America, North Mankato, MN.

Table of Contents

Fox Pups and Wolf Pups!	4
Snouts and Ears	8
Pup Lives	14
Who Is Cuter?	20
Glossary	22
To Learn More	23
Index	24

Fox Pups and Wolf Pups!

Baby foxes and baby wolves share a name. They are called pups!

fox pups

wolf pups

Both pups are born in **dens**. They have **siblings**. Both pups are cute!

siblings

den

Snouts and Ears

Fox pups mostly have red fur and black legs. Wolf pups are mostly brown and gray.

Fox pups have thin **snouts**. Wolf pups have wider snouts.

Fox pups have tall, pointed ears. Wolf pups have shorter ears.

Pup Lives

Mom and dad bring fox pups food. A **pack** cares for wolf pups.

pack

Pups play! Fox pups stand on their back legs. They push. Wolf pups do not.

Both pups bark. But only wolf pups learn to **howl**. Which pup is cuter?

howling

barking

19

Who Is Cuter?

tall, pointed ears

thin snout

mostly red fur and black legs

Baby Fox

cared for by mom and dad

stands on back legs and pushes

barks

Glossary

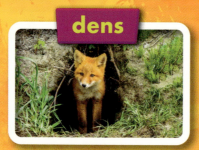

dens

sheltered places

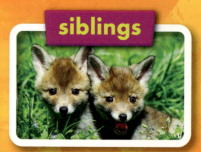

siblings

brothers and sisters

howl

to make a long, loud cry

snouts

the noses and mouths of some animals

pack

a group of wolves that lives and hunts together

To Learn More

AT THE LIBRARY

Cutest Animals on the Planet. Washington, D.C.: National Geographic, 2021.

Leaf, Christina. *Baby Foxes.* Minneapolis, Minn.: Bellwether Media, 2022.

Neuenfeldt, Elizabeth. *Baby Wolves.* Minneapolis, Minn.: Bellwether Media, 2023.

ON THE WEB

FACTSURFER

Factsurfer.com gives you a safe, fun way to find more information.

1. Go to www.factsurfer.com.
2. Enter "baby fox or baby wolf" into the search box and click 🔍.
3. Select your book cover to see a list of related content.

Index

bark, 18, 19
colors, 8, 9
dad, 14
dens, 6, 7
ears, 12
food, 14
foxes, 4
fur, 8, 9
howl, 18, 19
legs, 8, 9, 16
mom, 14
name, 4

pack, 14, 15
play, 16
push, 16
siblings, 6, 7
snouts, 10, 11
stand, 16
wolves, 4

The images in this book are reproduced through the courtesy of: Volodymyr Burdiak, front cover (fox), pp. 8-9; Don Johnston_MA / Alamy Stock Photo/ Alamy, front cover (wolf), p. 22 (howl); cynoclub/ Adobe Stock, p. 3 (fox); GlobalP, p. 3 (wolf); Jim Cumming pp. 4-5; Copyright Michael Cummings/ Getty Images, pp. 5, 9; Janet Horton / Alamy Stock Photo/ Alamy, pp. 6-7, 21 (does not stand and push); Jack Nevitt, p. 7; Design Pics/ Getty Images, pp. 10-11; Robert Adamec, p. 11; DragoNika/ Adobe Stock, pp. 12-13; slowmotiongli/ Getty Images/ iStock, pp. 13, 22 (siblings); Arterra Picture Library / Alamy Stock Photo/ Alamy, pp. 14-15; All Canada Photos / Alamy Stock Photo/ Alamy, p. 15; Carlos Carreno/ Getty Images/ Alamy, pp. 16-17, 20 (stands on back legs and pushes), 20 (barks); Imagebroker / Alamy Stock Photo/ Alamy, p. 17; Jason Hahn / Alamy Stock Photo/ Alamy pp. 18-19; Brezina, p. 19; Eric Isselee, pp. 20 (fox), 21 (wolf); Richard Seeley, p. 20 (cared for by mom and dad); Ronald Wittek / Alamy Stock Photo/ Alamy, p. 21 (cared for by pack); John Pitcher, p. 21 (barks and howls); Dee Carpenter/ Adobe Stock, p. 22 (dens); Michal Martinek, p. 22 (pack); Karel Bartik, p. 22 (snouts).

24